COUNTDOWN

TO A **FAIRER** WORLD

Compiled by **Tom Genrich**

GW00691616

COUNTDOWN
TO A FAIRER WORLD

First published in the UK in 2005 by
New Internationalist™ Publications Ltd
55 Rectory Road
Oxford OX4 1BW, UK.
www.newint.org

Compiled by Tom Genrich.

Design: New Internationalist.

Printed on recycled paper by T J International Ltd, Padstow, Cornwall,
who hold environmental accreditation ISO 14001.

British Library Cataloguing-in-Publication Data.
A catalogue record for this book is available from the British Library.

ISBN 1 904456 28 6

Introduction

Numbers surround us, marking out our lives and informing us about the world. Actually it is not numbers that do these things but rather we humans who use numbers to put order into our lives, to measure, count, compare and compute.

We can use numbers to tell more or less any story we want. One person might want to argue that the free market economy has brought benefit to humanity – and cite as proof the rise in overall wealth while conveniently omitting to mention how small a proportion of this wealth trickles down to the poorest. Another might point to booming international trade figures. One person might use these statistics in support of their argument that the globalized free market is bringing great benefit to humanity. Another, meanwhile, might cite the same figures as proof of the environmental unsustainability of our modern consumer world.

This little book is unashamedly biased in the numbers it lists: it aims to offer fuel to the fire of all those arguing for a fairer world. It tells you, for example, how many landmines still litter the earth; how many kids die every day from poverty; how many mobile phones we chuck away each year and how many species are threatened with extinction.

But **Countdown** also charts some of the major improvements in people's lives. Smallpox has been eradicated and polio should soon follow. World average life expectancy has gone up, despite the recent setbacks in Southern Africa. The land under organic production continues to rise, as does the sale of organic and fair trade items. And the ivory-billed woodpecker – declared extinct in 1920 – was seen alive and well in February 2004.

The book offers a fascinating insight into the planet through figures from 34.5 trillion down to minus 500 million. Here are hundreds of facts to set you thinking and spur you to action: campaigns and action groups are listed by many of the entries, and the reference section at the back lists more organizations and resources. The countdown to a fairer world starts now...

NOTE: Exchange rate of US$1.83 = £1.00 used throughout.
1 billion has nine zeroes in the American system, as used in this book (1,000 million) and also used now in Britain. The French/German system refers to a billion as a million million (with 12 zeroes) – the equivalent of an American/British trillion (also 12 zeroes).

$34,491,000,000,000
($34.5 trillion)

– the total global income in 2003, 80% ($27.7 trillion) of which is earned in high-income countries that contain just 15% of the world's population.[1]

$13,000,000,000,000
($13 trillion)

…is the approximate income of the world's seven richest countries that is based on the unsustainable consumption of fossil fuels.[2]

$956,000,000,000
($956 BILLION)

– total global military spending in 2003.[3]
Protest against military spending and weapons

See the **Campaign Against Arms Trade** which works for
the ending of the international arms trade, as well as for
progressive demilitarization within arms-producing countries.
www.caat.org.uk/

nearly $500,000,000,000 ($500 billion)

…or almost a quarter of all Third World debt, results from loans that were used to prop up dictators.[4]

$390,000,000,000 ($390 BILLION)

…could have been raised in 2002 alone by the 'Tobin Tax' on currency speculation set at just 0.1%. This sum was seven times the total development aid at the time.[5]

$190,000,000,000 ($190 billion)

...is the estimated wealth, in today's US dollars, of the richest person ever: John D Rockefeller.[6]

$167,000,000,000 ($167 billion)

...is the cost to the US of the Iraq war (as of May 2005). This could have fully funded all global anti-hunger programmes for 6 years, all AIDS programmes for 15 years and all basic immunizations for every child in the world for 51 years.[7]

See the constantly updated figure online at www.costofwar.com

$110,000,000,000 ($110 BILLION)

...were spent on fast food by Americans in 2000.[8]

See McLibel Spotlight for the campaign against McDonald's at www.mcspotlight.org/

106,000,000,000 (106 billion)

...births since the dawn of the human race, which would mean 5.8 per cent of all people ever born are alive today.

See how this figure was computed at **Population Reference Bureau www.prb.org**

$88,000,000,000 (£48 billion)

…is the estimated cost of cleaning up the nuclear legacy just in Britain. This is expected to take over 100 years.[9]

$69,029,000,000 ($69 billion)

– the total official development assistance given by rich countries in 2003, which represented just 0.25% of their gross national income, compared with the UN minimum of 0.7% of income.[10]

$46,000,000,000
($46 billion)

...is the wealth of the richest person living, Microsoft founder Bill Gates, as of 2004.[11]

If you're interested in countering the growing Microsoft domination of everything digital, see the **Boycott Microsoft** campaign at **www.vcnet.com/bms/**

46,000,000,000 (46 billion)

…broiler chickens are reared for their meat in the world every year, 5.5 billion of them in the EU. The majority are intensively farmed and kept in windowless, barren and crowded sheds, holding tens of thousands of birds for their brief six-week lives.

Take action at Compassion in World Farming
www.ciwf.org.uk/

$40,000,000,000
($40 BILLION)

– the total spent on food advertising in the world in 1999 – $16 billion could have funded all the UN's anti-hunger programmes for a year.[12]

$30,000,000,000
($30 billion)

– the estimated personal wealth of the world's richest monarch, King Fahd Bin Abdulaziz Alsaud of Saudi Arabia, in 2001. His dollars primarily come from oil, property and investments.[13]

$27,000,000,000
($27 billion)

...worth of economic losses are incurred each year in Africa due to war.[14]

Outraged? Contact Control Arms campaign
www.controlarms.org

15,000,000,000
(15 billion)

...years have elapsed since the planetary 'Big Bang'.

$14,000,000,000
(£8 billion)

...is donated to charities every year by British individuals.[15]

$14,000,000,000
(11 billion euros)

...are spent each year by Austria, France and Switzerland on deaths, illnesses, treatments and lost work hours due to road pollution.[16]

$10,000,000,000
($10 billion)

– the value of sales of organically grown foods in Europe in 2002, up 8 per cent from the previous year.[17]

$6,500,000,000
($6.5 billion)

…of aid had been pledged by April 2005 to the countries affected by the December 2004 tsunami.[18]

$4,800,000,000
(£2.6 billion)

…was lost by companies in 2002 as British consumers made an ethical decision to switch or boycott brands.[19]

2,692,200,000
(2.7 BILLION)

…people – the combined populations of China, India, Russia, Mexico, Ukraine and South Africa – have together produced less carbon dioxide pollution since 1950 than has the US, with its population of 291,000,000 (0.3 billion).[20]

2,000,000,000
(2 billion)

...people in the world are illiterate.[21]

$1,150,000,000
(£628 million)

– the total cost of London's Millennium Dome to the British taxpayer up to the end of 2000, or about $3.1 million (£1.7 million) for every one of the 365 days that it stayed open.[22]

1,000,000,000
(1 billion)

– microbes are contained in 1 teaspoon of healthy soil.[23]

– people on the planet are illegal squatters.[24]

– people use mobile phones, or more than 1 in 7 people on earth.[25]

– children live in poverty, almost every second child in the world.[26]

– dollars are spent on agricultural subsidies in the US and Europe every day.[27]

760,000,000

– the number of international tourist arrivals during 2004.[28]

$660,000,000

...would make solar power economically competitive for electricity production. This is just 0.5% of the money spent on oil exploration in 1998 alone.[29]

639,000,000

…small arms and light weapons already exist in the world – 1 for every 10 people. An additional 8 million are manufactured every year.[30]

600,000,000

…tonnes of CO_2 are produced each year by commercial aviation, over 93 kg for every man, woman and child. Every 10 kilometres of a long-haul flight creates about 1 kg per passenger, all contributing to global warming.[31]

531,000,000

...is the number of cars in the world, or 1 for every 11 of us.[32]

$325,000,000

– the estimated cost of decommissioning just 1 nuclear reactor in the US (1998 $).[33]

200,000,000– 215,000,000

…landmines are still in or on the ground, particularly in Afghanistan, Cambodia, Iraq, Iran, Egypt and Angola, lying in wait for children, women, men and livestock.[34]

Help remove them through organizations like **Mine Advisory Group** www.mag.org.uk or **Medical Association for the Prevention of War (Australia)** www.mapw.org.au

$200,000,000

...are spent each year by the British Government on removing pesticides from drinking water. Put another way, that is about a quarter of what British farmers spend on buying them in the first place.[35]

Find out more about pesticides from **Pesticides Action Network** www.pan-international.org/

160,000,000

…years ago was when the earliest surviving species of tree, the maidenhair (Ginkgo biloba) of Zhejiang, China, first appeared.[36]

157,000,000

…tons of sugar and sweeteners are consumed worldwide every year, a global per capita consumption of 245 calories a day.[37]

$128,000,000
(£70 million)

...per week is given to the UK's 9.14 million children as pocket money.[38]

123,000,000

– the membership of The International Confederation of Free Trade Unions in 2002. The union was set up in 1949 and has 215 affiliated organizations in 145 countries and territories on all five continents. Some 43 million of its 123 million members are women. The confederation aims to protect workers' rights and supports the eradication of forced and child labour, the promotion of equal rights for working women, and safe working environments.[39]

$112,000,000

– the estimated annual revenue Burma's military regime pocketed from timber sales in the 1990s.[40]

100,000,000

– the number of bicycles produced in 2000.[41]

...years ago, the Leatherback turtle swam with the dinosaurs. Now the turtle is threatened with extinction as a result of longline fishing (used to catch swordfish).[42]

Don't eat swordfish! Help save the turtle at: **Save the Leatherback Campaign** at www.savetheleatherback.com

59,000,000

...hectares worldwide have been planted with GM crops (as of 2003).[43]

Join the **Bite Back** campaign against US pressure on the World Trade Organization to allow GM products into the global market – **www.bite-back.org**

46,000,000

– the number of customers served each day in McDonald's. It has 30,000 restaurants in 119 countries.[44]

$44,000,000
(£24 MILLION)

...per year: the earnings of British football icon David Beckham from his sports and advertising contracts.[45] That's $82 for every minute of every day of the year, or $82 by the time he has finished reading this snippet.

5,000,000

...names are on the US Master Terror Watchlist: that's 1 in every 1,300 people on the planet.[55]

$5,000,000
or just under

– one of the highest single sales ever recorded on eBay, in US dollars, when a 12-seater Gulfstream II business jet was auctioned in 2001.[56]

3,000,000

...Australian households say they grow fruit or vegetables in their garden (2004).[57]

...people rallied at the largest anti-Iraq war demonstration in February 2003, in Rome, Italy. Millions more demonstrated in nearly 600 cities worldwide: 1.3 million in Barcelona, Spain, 1 million in London, England, and 500,000 people in Melbourne and Sydney, Australia, joining the biggest marches since the Vietnam War protests.[58]

1,500,000

...people have been displaced by the 2004
Indian Ocean tsunami.[59]

1,000,000

...people will not survive this week.[60]

– the number of employees of Wal-Mart Stores, the largest corporation in the world (April 2002).[61]

– the number of people in Canada in 2001 identifying themselves with an Aboriginal group or reporting themselves as a Registered or Treaty Indian or a member of an Indian Band or First Nation.[62]

884,647

…words in total are used by Shakespeare in his plays and sonnets, made up of 29,066 different forms.[63]

800,000

– the estimated number of Rwandans killed between April and June 1994 in the genocide. [64]

609,700

– the estimated resident Maori population in New Zealand/Aotearoa (2003). Total NZ population is 4 million.[65]

365,000

...US citizens die every year of problems related to poor diet and physical inactivity – more than from alcohol, microbial and toxic agents, car crashes, adverse reactions to prescribed drugs, suicide, incidents involving firearms, homicide, sexual conduct and all illicit drug use combined.[66]

300,000

– the estimated number of people killed by the December 2004 Indian Ocean tsunami.[67]

210,000

...cubic metres of radioactive waste are produced by nuclear power generation each year worldwide.[68]

150,000

...years ago modern humans developed in Africa. By 11,000 BCE, homo sapiens sapiens had spread around the globe. By 1968 humanity was travelling to other planets.[69]

$91,500
(£50,000)

...was spent by the department of the UK Deputy Prime Minister John Prescott on hiring pot plants for its offices. That's potted plants.[70]

73,000+

...Maori live in Australia.[71]

70,828

– the number of divorces in Canada in 2003.[72]

70,000+

...hours of your life are spent on your career, so choose well.

Try these: www.ethicalcareers.org, www.oneworld.net, www.gn.apc.org, www.devnetjobs.org.uk, www.sgr.org.uk

Countdown

29,158

– the number of children under 5 dying every single day as a result of extreme poverty.[73]

Join the action to **make poverty history** at **www.makepovertyhistory.org/**

Countdown

28,900

...was the percentage increase in the land area farmed using sustainable-agriculture practices in Asia, Latin America and Africa between 1991 and 2001.[74]

$28,000

...is the average gross national income per capita of industrialized countries – 200 times that of Guinea-Bissau.[75]

20,000-25,000

...genes were found in the human genome sequence, which only a decade ago was thought to contain at least four times that number.[76]

$22,360

...is the cost of an average US wedding. The net financial loss to the couple, after the value of the gifts has been factored in, is over $13,000.[77]

15,503

– the number of threatened species (animals and plants) in 2004.[78]

10,000

...square kilometres is the size of the world's biggest iceberg, B15, that calved from the Ross Ice Shelf in 2000. This is 2,000,000 times the largest estimate of the iceberg that sank the Titanic in 1912.[79]

8,212

...MWe is the total output of the world's largest nuclear power station, Kashiwazaki Kariwa in Japan.[80]

6,443

– the number of Blockbuster stores worldwide. The US firm is the world's largest video retailer, with a 30% market share.[81]

6,300+

...people died from the poisonous cloud of methyl isocyanate which escaped from a Union Carbide pesticide plant near Bhopal, India, in 1984. As many as 20,000 more are estimated to have died since then. The company paid $470 million to the Indian Government in 1999 as compensation for the families, but some has still not been disbursed.[82]

5,500

…years ago the first-ever depiction of the wheel was made by the Sumerians, who are credited with inventing it. Among other things, they used it for combat chariots.[83]

5,048

– the number of indigenous prisoners in Australia (21% of the prison population), June 2004. Indigenous people were 11 times more likely than non-indigenous people to be imprisoned.[84]

4,000+

...chemicals make up tobacco smoke, including compounds otherwise found in insecticides, fuel, solvents, cleaners and paint stripper.[85]

3,900

– the number of children who die each day because they lack access to safe drinking water and adequate sanitation.[86]

Countdown

3,731

...women in the UK had their breasts augmented in 2004; 2,417 had them reduced, making these two procedures the most common cosmetic surgery for UK women.[87]

2002

– the year the South African Government took action to discourage use and careless disposal of plastic bags, prompting a 90-per-cent reduction in use. [88]

1,000

– cubic metres of water, or about 1,000 tons, are required to produce 1 ton of wheat.[89]

– cubic metres of water available per person per year means that a country is said to be 'water-stressed'; anything less is a 'serious water crisis'.[90]

– dollars is the maximum cost of clearing up 1 landmine, up to 333 times higher than its production cost.

Contact groups such as Mines Advisory Group www.mag.org.uk; International Campaign to Ban Landmines www.icbl.org; and Medical Association for the Prevention of War Australia www.mapw.org.au

996

…men and women were beatified and another 447 canonized by Pope John Paul II – which is comparable to the numbers for the four previous centuries combined.[91]

955

…people are in immigration detention in Australia, April 2005.[92]

897

...is the number of cigarettes per person manufactured in 2002 – down from 913 in 2001.[93]

800

...is New Zealand/Aotearoa's annual quota of people classified as refugees by the United Nations High Commissioner for Refugees (UNHCR).[94]

700

– the percentage increase in humanity's energy footprint* between 1961 and 2001.[95]

*calculated as the area required to provide, or absorb the waste from, fossil fuels (coal, oil, and natural gas), fuelwood, nuclear energy, and hydropower.

555

– the first three digits of a typical phone number in a Hollywood film (not allocated).

500

...years are needed to create 2.5 cm of topsoil – 50,000 square km of arable land is lost per year to wind and water erosion, salination, sodication and desertification. [96]

$400+

...is the debt per person – for every man, woman and child – in the Majority World.[97]

Support the **Jubilee 2000** campaign to drop the debt at **www.jubilee2000uk.org** and the **Trade Justice movement** at **www.foei.org/**

385%

– Zimbabwe's inflation rate in 2003, the highest in the world. Consumer prices increased by five times.[98]

362

...nose jobs were given to UK men in 2004, making rhinoplasty their top cosmetic-surgery procedure of that year.[99]

338

– the number of Somalians that it would take to earn the gross national income of one Luxembourgeois.[100]

– the number of drink brands sold by Coca-Cola in over 200 countries. More than 70% of the company's income comes from outside the US.[101]

246

...compounds and viruses are now officially identified as carcinogens by the US Department of Health and Human Services, including hepatitis, lead, naphthalene (as used in mothballs) and certain compounds formed when meat or eggs are cooked or grilled at high temperatures.[102]

200+

...years is how long it would take to clear Cambodia of landmines at 2001 removal rates.[103]

See Cambodia Mine Action Centre at www.cmac.org; Landmine Action www.landmineaction.org/ and The Halo Trust www.halotrust.org/

$210

...is the per capita annual income in Mozambique (2003). This is $90 shy of the lowest possible cost of antiretroviral therapy for 1 person with HIV/AIDS for 1 year. Mozambique has over 1 million HIV-positive citizens.[104]

200+

...cities worldwide have more than 2 million inhabitants.

193

…countries currently exist in the world (including the Vatican and Taiwan) and roughly 6,800 languages. Some 96% of these languages are spoken by just 4% of the planet's population.[105]

160

…is the percentage increase in hydro-meteorological disasters since 1975.[106]

156

...US parliamentarians voted against President George W Bush's Iraq war resolution on 11 October 2002, or over 1 in 4.[107]

145

...is the percentage of the recommended daily energy intake that the average American consumes: 3,636 kcal a day. By contrast, 127 units of energy are required to transport 1 unit of lettuce energy from California to London.[108]

130+

...Afghani refugees on the rescue ship Tampa were accepted for settlement in New Zealand/ Aotearoa in 2001, after Australia made it difficult for them to stay there.[109]

115

– the number of refrigerators per 100 households in the US; the comparable figure for India is 12.[110]

100+

– products are now certified 'Fairtrade', such as coffee and tea, bananas, chocolate and cocoa, sugar and honey.[111]

– of Scotland's chip shops sell deep-fried Mars bars, up to 200 pieces a week each.[112]

100

– per cent of the human body will be transplantable or replaceable by 2030, given sufficient funds.[113]

– per cent of women in Barbados are literate. The lowest female literacy rate in the world is Niger's 9%. Only just over 1 in 6 of all adults in Niger can read and write.[114]

– million sharks are killed each year to feed world appetite for shark meat and shark fin soup.[115]

98%

…is the reduction in average visibility in Mexico City since 1940, due to pollution.[116]

96%

– the fall, from 1987 to 1996, of Canada's production of ozone-depleting substances (from 28 kilotonnes to 1 kilotonne per year). From 1988 to 1995, global production of these substances fell by 77%.[117]

95%

...of the world's production of nutmeg comes from Indonesia and the Caribbean island of Grenada. Nutmeg essential oil is used in Coca-Cola among other products. Excess consumption of the spice can lead to nutmeg psychosis.[118]

91%+

...of the world's GM hectares are used for growing Monsanto products.[119]

See information on Monsanto at **Corporate Watch** www.corporatewatch.org.uk and the **Organic Food Association**'s campaign at www.purefood.org/campaign

90%

– of the world's GM crops are grown in just two countries, the US and Argentina.

– of the EU's agricultural budget is spent subsidising industrial rather than organic agriculture.[120]

– of the world's HIV-positive people live in developing countries.[121]

– of conflict-related casualties since 1990 have been civilians.[122]

$90

...a month donated to OXFAM will pay a Kenyan trainee teacher's salary.

89%

– the percentage of households in Australia purchasing environmentally friendly products (EFPs) in 2004. This was similar to 2001 (90%).[123]

83%

...of Tanzania's Kilimanjaro glacier has disappeared in a century, reducing it to 2 square kilometres.[124]

80%

...of farmers in developing countries do not need to change their methods to be certified organic.[125]

...of all people executed in the US since 1976 died in the South, which has just a third of the US's population and continues to have the highest murder rate in the country. So much for deterrence.[126]

...of all coltan, an extremely heat-resistant superconductor used in cellphones, comes from the Democratic Republic of Congo...

– where its mining often uses forced labour in hazardous conditions, and devastates habitat and wildlife.[127]

...of the world's agricultural land suffers from moderate to severe erosion.[128]

76%

...of Canada's grain consumption is used for animal feed (1994).[129]

75%

– the increase in total worldwide organic food and drink sales over just three years, to about $17.5 billion (1997-2000). This is still only 3% of total retail sales, but is predicted to grow by around 20% per year.[130]

...of EU agricultural land is used to grow animal feed.[131]

...is the proportion of the world's population that is less comfortable than you if there is food in your fridge, clothing on your back, a roof over your head, and a bed for you to sleep in.[132]

70

...square metres is the total surface area of the lung of an average adult human.[133]

68%

...of the US's total stock of chemical weapons still remain to be disposed of under the 1990 International Chemical Weapons Convention – by 2012.[134]

62%

…of men think technology makes it easier to cheat on their partners; 33% of women think they have the upper hand in their current sexual relationship.[135]

58

…is the factor by which the risk of Iraqis dying a violent death increased after the US-led invasion of Iraq in March 2003.[136]

57%

...of Australians (8.6 million) aged 18 years and over stated that they were concerned about environmental problems. However, this was down from 1992's figure of 75%.[137]

51

...of the 100 largest economies in the world are corporations, not countries.[138]

50

– the number of expressions for 'snow' and 'ice' in the Canadian Inuit language Inuktitut. It has no word for 'pollution' or 'contaminant', although plenty of both now exist in the form of heavy-metal and chemical contamination of the marine food chain.[139]

– the average percentage reduction in child and infant mortality rates in developing countries since 1960.[140]

…kilos of hazardous waste per person are produced every year, at a minimum.[141]

…per cent of Canadians aged 25 to 44 felt trapped in a daily routine in 1998.[142]

48

...Canadians in every 100 are internet users; the comparable figure in Australia is 56; in New Zealand/Aotearoa, 52; in Britain, 42 (2003); 2 per 100 in Bhutan and under 1 per 100 in the Central African Republic.[143]

47%

...of Australian households engaged in water conservation practices in 2004; 74% had dual flush toilets while 44% had reduced-flow shower heads.[144]

43%

...of human-made carbon emissions come from electricity production, 25% from transport and 19% from industry.[145]

40

– the percentage by which global populations of terrestrial, marine and freshwater species declined between 1970 and 2000.[146]

– the size in hectares of the world's largest natural asphalt deposit, Pitch Lake in Trinidad.[147]

– the number of cars required to carry the same number of people as 1 double-decker bus.[148]

38

...US states have the death penalty. The 12 which do not are: Alaska, Hawaii, Iowa, Maine, Massachusetts, Michigan, Minnesota, North Dakota, Rhode Island, Vermont, West Virginia, and Washington DC.[149]

33%

...of all known amphibian species are at risk of extinction. Amphibians are considered good indicator species for environmental degradation (think canary in a mineshaft).[150]

– the decline in global per capita water supply since 1970.[151]

32

– the original length, in seconds, of Qatar's national anthem before its recent expansion.[152]

30+ years

– the median age of New Zealand women having babies in 2003.[153]

30

– the number of hours per week spent on childcare by 16% of Canadian women aged 15 and over, more than twice the proportion among men (7%).[154]

– the number of professional orchestras in Finland.[155]

27

– the percentage by which the US divorce rate is higher in Republican states than in Democratic ones.[156]

26%

– of all regimes were authoritarian in 1995, down from 68% in 1975.[157]

– of the world's oil, coal and natural gas are consumed by the US, which has 0.05% of the world's population (2001).[158]

25%

...of the world's population live in areas where the level of air pollution exceeds WHO safety standards.[159]

...of the world's mammals are under significant threat of extinction.[160]

24%

– the growth in the average book collection per library in Canada between 1994 and 1999. Using a local library is still a part of Canadian life; the level of borrowing activity grew by 5%.[161]

22

...years have been lost off the life expectancy of Zimbabweans, now at 33 years, since 1970. The same statistic is 16 in Botswana and 14 in Lesotho. All of these countries have estimated HIV/AIDS prevalence rates of at least 1 in 4.[162]

21

...is the widely accepted number of senses that humans have: light and colour (vision); hearing; smell; sweet, salt, sour, bitter (taste); pain; balance, joint position, body movement; hot and cold; blood pressure, blood oxygen content, cerebrospinal fluid pH, plasma osmotic pressure (thirst), artery-vein glucose difference (hunger), and lung inflation.[163]

...countries have been bombed by the US military since the Second World War.

20

– the number of years since global consumption began to exceed the planet's biocapacity.[164]

– the percentage by which 2001 levels of global consumption of the planet's biological resources such as agricultural land, fishing grounds and forests exceed their availability.[165]

– the percentage of young New Zealanders who identify with more than 1 ethnicity.[166]

18

...countries had cases of female genital mutilation or cutting between 1998 and 2003.[167]

16

...per cent of the world's annual production of the greenhouse gas methane comes from flatulent livestock.[168]

15.4%

...of the UK's children live in poverty.[169]

15

...countries still produced landmines in mid-2003.[170] Of these, India and Pakistan are actively engaged in new production of anti-personnel mines.

– the factor by which Africa is bigger than Greenland, despite the two landmasses looking the same size on traditional maps such as the Mercator, with their distortion of size favouring the Northern hemisphere.[171]

– the percentage of women representatives in the world's lower houses of parliament.[172]

$13

– the amount spent by the Majority World on debt repayment for every $1 that it receives in grants.[173]

every
12 to 15

...minutes for up to five days is the mating frequency of lions.[174]

12

– the number per human inhabitant of sheep in New Zealand/Aotearoa, rats in New York City, and (at the very least) snowshoe hares in Canada.[175]

– the percentage of birds worldwide under significant threat of extinction.[176]

11.87

...metres is the annual rainfall of the world's wettest place, Meghalaya in India.[177]

11

...per cent of Sweden's arable land is cultivated organically, the highest percentage in the world.[178]

– the number of countries where landmines were still used in 2003: Burma, Burundi, Columbia, India, Iraq, Pakistan, Philippines, Russia (Chechnya), Somalia, Sudan and Nepal.

...February 2004, was the day that Gene Sparling of Hot Springs, Arkansas, saw the ivory-billed woodpecker, which had been declared extinct in 1920.[179]

10.2-14.7

...is the real cost, in US cents per unit, of nuclear electricity once all external costs such as subsidies, disposal, etc have been factored in. This compares to 2.4-8.7 cents per unit for hydropower and 4.05-6.25 for wind power.[180]

10

...times more of Ireland's central government expenditure goes on health and education combined than on defence.[181]

– the minimum amount, in centimetres, that the global mean sea level rose during the 20th century.[182]

– the factor by which this increase is bigger than that of the previous 3 millennia.[183]

– the percentage shrinkage of the world's snow cover since the 1960s.[184]

– the number of animal species known to have become extinct since the arrival of the first European settlers in northern North America.[185]

9

…countries have nuclear capability, according to the International Atomic Energy Agency: US, Russia, UK, France, China, India, Pakistan, North Korea and Israel.[186] Four of these countries spend between 3 and 9 times more on defence than on health and education combined: India, Pakistan, China and Russia.[187]

8

…times more of the US's central government expenditure goes on defence than on education (1992-2002).[188]

– the percentage of the fuel mix in all petrol cars that could be biofuel, ie derived from wheat, straw, sugar beet, forest trimmings, etc, without any impairment. In Britain, this could save substantially more in carbon emissions than the Government's entire 10-year transport plan.[189]

7

– the number of years by which average life expectancy has increased worldwide since 1970.[190]

– the percentage by which tropical forest cover on the planet fell between 1990 and 2000.[191]

– the number of times that the 'human lightning conductor', park ranger Roy C Sullivan of Virginia, has been struck by lightning.[192]

6.6

– the percentage reduction in the average fuel economy of US passenger cars between 1987 and 1997. At the same time, there was a 33% increase in the average miles travelled per person in the US. And the US population grew by a few million.[193]

5

– the factor by which grain use increases if a person is fed for 1 year on a meat-based diet rather than a grain-based diet.[194]

– the number of Earths required to support the global use of resources if everyone had an eco footprint the size of the average US consumer.[195]

...football-field equivalents of forest are cut down every 5 seconds.[196]

...of the 5 permanent members of the UN Security Council fill the 4 top spots on the list of the world's suppliers of major conventional weapons. The 5th member, China, comes 9th on the list.[197]

...countries in the world have longer life expectancies for men than for women: the Maldives, Nepal, Zambia and Zimbabwe.[198]

less than 4

...days is all it takes for the average tourist to use as much water as a villager in the developing world in a whole year.[199]

3·75

...average sunshine hours per day were recorded in Britain in 2004. The Australian average is 6-10, the South African 8-10 and the Canadian 6 hours per day.[200]

3-5

– kilograms of wild fish are needed to produce just 1 kg of farmed salmon.[201] Not only does salmon farming produce as much sewage as 15 city-dwellers for every ton of salmon, the fish will also contain up to 16 times the levels of carcinogenic PCBs found in wild salmon.[202]

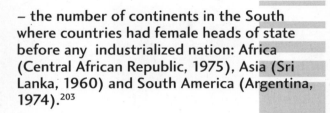

3

– the number of continents in the South where countries had female heads of state before any industrialized nation: Africa (Central African Republic, 1975), Asia (Sri Lanka, 1960) and South America (Argentina, 1974).[203]

– inhabitants per square kilometre live in Australia, the least densely populated of the inhabited continents. Monaco has 16.[204]

– the number of the richest people in the world combined that have more wealth than the 48 poorest nations.[205]

– the cost in US dollars of making the cheapest landmine.[206]

2.5

...bicycles are produced worldwide for
every 1 car.[207]

See **Friends of the Earth**'s transport campaigns at
www.foei.org

2.4

…kilograms of methane are produced by Canadian cattle each year for every kilogram of beef that Canadians eat.[208]

Cut out or eat less meat – see www.vegsoc.org & www.vegansociety.com (UK), www.americanvegan.org, www.ivu.org/vuna (US); www.veg.ca (Canada); www.veganaustralia.org (Aus), www.ivu.org/nzvs/ & www.veganz.pl.net (NZ)

...devastating infectious diseases will have been eradicated worldwide if the World Health Organization meets its targets: smallpox (1980) and polio (2005).[209]

...US dollars is what almost half the world's population has to live on per day.[210]

– the number of major greenhouse-gas emission countries that have refused to ratify the Kyoto Treaty on climate control, despite signing it: the US and Australia.

– the number of countries that have not ratified the Convention of the Rights of Children: Somalia and the US.[211]

– the number of British schools, both of them faith schools and city academies, that teach creationism.[212]

...per cent of the electricity used by a light bulb is converted into light, the rest into heat.[213]

...per cent of the world's electricity consumption could be saved if appliances not in use were switched off, rather than left on standby.[214]

...per cent of the earth's surface is covered by rainforests, yet they are home to some 40 to 50 per cent of all life forms on our planet – as many as 30 million species of plants, animals and insects.[215]

1-10

...centimetres per year is the average speed both of fingernail growth and of tectonic plate movement.[216]

1.82

...watts per capita of solar power is generated by Switzerland, the highest solar usage in the world; Germany has the second highest usage, with 0.71 watts per capita.[217]

1.2

...hectares is the largest known tree canopy area, that of the great banyan (*Ficus benghalensis*), in the Indian Botanical Garden, Calcutta.[218]

$1

– if there was an endless line of $1 bills laid end to end... and you began traveling along this line picking up dollar bills on 13 March 1986 (the day Microsoft went public), and you wished to accumulate wealth at the same rate Bill Gates has since that date, you would need to travel that line of bills picking them up at 16.61 mph/ 26.74 kph.

1

...person every minute is killed with conventional weapons. 15 new arms are manufactured for sale in that same minute.[219]

– the percentage of global freshwater that is available for use as a renewable resource.[220]

– is the number of people it takes to change the world.

$0.6°C$

– the degree by which the average global temperature at the Earth's surface has warmed since the late 19th century.[221]

...of 1 per cent of the UK's annual rainfall, if captured, could provide enough water to flush all UK toilets for the year. If all toilets were set up to provide reduced flushes, a quarter would suffice.[222]

– the reduction in journey times in central London since the introduction of the congestion charge in 2003.

– the increase in bus usage in London's congestion-charge zone.[223]

More

...live coverage of the 2004 Democratic national convention was shown on Al-Jazeera than any of the major commercial US networks.[224]

...money was earned by the UK, the US and France from selling arms to Majority World countries than they gave those countries in aid (1998-2001).[225]

Zero

– the greenhouse gas CO_2 that is produced per person per kilometre of walking or cycling. This compares with 75 grammes per person in mass transit/public transport that is three-quarters full; 275g in air travel; and up to 425g for the solo driver of the largest model SUVs.[226]

Countdown

-53°C

– the temperature of the Don Juan Pond in Wright Valley, Antarctica, which is so salty that it remains liquid even when it is this cold. [227]

-70 °C (-94 °F)

– the lowest temperature in the world's coldest inhabited village, Oymyakon in Siberia, Russia. [228]

−500

million years

– dating of the oldest footprints in the world, those of the 1-foot-long giant woodlouse, in Ontario, Canada.[229]

REFERENCES

1 *World Bank World Development Report 2005*. 2 Simms, 'Going Down in History', NI 342, Jan/Feb 2002. 3 Stockholm International Peace Research Institute (SIPRI). 4 Ellwood, *The No-Nonsense Guide to Globalization*, Verso/NI 2001. 5 Culver, 'Time for Tobin', NI 342. 6 *The Guinness Book of Records* www.guinnessworldrecords. com 7 National Priorities Project, www.costofwar.com 8 Guinness op cit. 9 Greenpeace www.greenpeace.org; *Nuclear Engineering International* magazine 'Creative clean-up', November 2004 and 'Clean-up authority gets power for the UK', April 2005 www.neimagazine.com 10 UN Development Programme, *Human Development Report 2004*. 11 Guinness op cit. 12 Millstone and Lang, *The Atlas of Food: Who Eats What, Where and Why*, Earthscan 2003; and UN Food and Agriculture Organization. www.fao.org 13 Guinness op cit. 14 NI 367; www.controlarms.org 15 www.prospects.ac.uk 16 de Bartillack and Retallack, *Stop*, Seuil 2003. 17 Worldwatch Institute, *State of the World 2004*, Norton 2004, www.worldwatch.org 18 Voice of America News 'Clinton: Tough Times Ahead for Tsunami-Hit Region' 25 April 2005 www.voanews.com 19 Khaneka, *Do the Right Things*, NI 2004. 20 Shiva, *Water Wars*, Pluto Press 2002. 21 Meadows, *State of the Village Report*, www.odt.org 22 National Audit Office report, *The Millennium Dome*, 9 November 2000. www.nao.org.uk 23 *The Ecologist*, Dec 2004/Jan 2005. 24 Neuwirth, *Shadow Cities: A Billion Squatters, a New Urban World*, Routledge 2004. 25 Worldwatch Institute, *Vital Signs, 2002-2003*, Earthscan 2002. 26 UNICEF, *The State of the World's Children 2005*; and UNAIDS www.unaids.org 27 Oxfam www. oxfam.org 28 World Tourism Organization www.world-tourism.org 29 Ravetz, *The No-Nonsense Guide to Science*, Verso/NI 2005. 30 www.controlarms.org 31 www. airportwatch.org.uk 32 de Bartillack and Retallack op cit.; Worldwatch Institute *State of the World 2004* op cit. 33 www.world-nuclear.org 34 UNICEF op cit. 35 Worldwatch Institute, *Vital Signs* op cit. 36 Guinness op cit. 37 Worldwatch Institute, *Vital Signs* op cit. 38 *Prospect*, Sept 2004. 39 Guinness op cit. 40 Worldwatch Institute, *Vital Signs* op cit. 41 Earth Policy Institute www.earth-policy.org 42 *The Ecologist* 26 Feb 2004 www.theecologist.org. 43 Worldwatch Institute, *State of the World 2004* op cit. 44 ibid. 45 www.salon.com 46 www.mongabay.com 47 Worldwatch Institute, *State of the World 2004* op cit. 48 Green Belt Movement www. greenbeltmovement.org 49 We Are What We Do, *Change the World for a Fiver*, Short Books 2004. 50 *World Refugee Survey 2001*, US Committee for Refugees; The Refugee Council of Australia www.refugeecouncil.org.au 51 Guinness op cit. 52 We Are What We Do op cit. 53 Statistics Canada www.statcan.ca 54 www.auctionbytes. com/cab/abn/y04/m04/i29/s02 55 NI 376. 56 *Silicon Valley/San Jose Business Journal*, 16 August 2001 sanjose.bizjournals.com 57 Australian Bureau of Statistics www.abs.gov.au 58 Guinness op cit. 59 en.wikipedia.org 60 Meadows op cit. 61 Guinness op cit. 62 Statistics Canada op cit. 63 www.worldwideorgs.org 64 http:// news.bbc.co.uk 65 New Zealand Government statistics www.population.govt.nz 66 US Food and Nutrition Service www.fns.usda.gov 67 http://geology.about.org 68 International Atomic Energy Agency www.iaea.org, and UK Government www.defra. gov.uk 69 'Homo sapiens', *Encyclopaedia Britannica*. 70 BBC Magazine News Quiz, 29 January 2005. 71 New Zealand Government op cit. 72 Statistics Canada op cit. 73 UNICEF op cit. 74 Pretty and Hine, 'Reducing Food Poverty with Sustainable Agriculture: A Summary of New Evidence' (2001), Centre for Environment and Society, University of Essex www2.essex.ac.uk 75 UNICEF op cit. and UNAIDS op cit. 76 Guinness op cit. 77 *Mother Jones*, Jan/Feb 2005. 78 IUCN Redlist www. redlist.org 79 www.landcareresearch.co.nz; and www.titanic-titanic.com/icebergs. shtml 80 Guinness op cit. 81 ibid. 82 ibid. and http://news.bbc.co.uk 83 'Wheel', *Encyclopaedia Britannica*. 84 Australian Bureau of Statistics op cit. 85 Ravetz op